KT-155-700

cavalier king charles spaniel

understanding and
caring for your breed

Written by
Lucy Koster

Pet Book Publishing Company

The Old Hen House, St Martin's Farm, Zeals, Warminster, Wiltshire, BA12 6NZ, United Kingdom.

Printed by Printworks Global Ltd., London & Hong Kong

All rights reserved. No part of this work may be reproduced, in any form or by any means, electronic or mechanical, including photocopying, recording or by any information storage and retrieval system, without the prior written permission of the publisher.

Copyright © Pet Book Publishing Company 2015.

Every reasonable care has been taken in the compilation of this publication. The Publisher and Author cannot accept liability for any loss, damage, injury or death resulting from the keeping of Cavalier King Charles Spaniels by user(s) of this publication, or from the use of any materials, equipment, methods or information recommended in this publication or from any errors or omissions that may be found in the text of this publication or that may occur at a future date, except as expressly provided by law.

The 'he' pronoun is used throughout this book instead of the rather impersonal 'it', however no gender bias is intended.

ISBN: 978-1-906305-67-3
ISBN: 1-906305-67-6

Acknowledgements

The publishers would like to thank the following for help with photography: Lucy Koster and Ellie Mordecai (Millhill).

Contents

Introducing the Cavalier

The Cavalier King Charles Spaniel is the perfect all rounder. As a 'spaniel' he is fearless, outgoing, fun, sporting and adventurous, and as a 'toy' breed he is small enough to live in an apartment and make do with a small amount exercise. Most of all, a Cavalier is renowned for his excellent temperament, which makes him an ideal family pet.

A dog for all ages

The Cavalier is one of the most adaptable of breeds, and he will fit in with many different lifestyles.

He can be very gentle and careful around small children, but he is also fun and playful with older children. He can be a wonderful comforter to anyone on their own, but he will also 'share himself out' around a family.

He will enjoy being active and going for long treks, or he will content himself with shorter outings and pottering around in the garden if his owners are getting on in years.

In all my years breeding Cavaliers, I have never known anyone to whom I've sold a puppy change from this breed to another – they may add a different breed, but always stick with a Cavalier no matter what!

Vive la différence

When people are discussing the breed, they frequently refer to the King Charles Cavalier or simply the King Charles but, in fact, there are two distinct breeds. At first glance, the King Charles Spaniel and the Cavalier King Charles Spaniel may look the same, but for those in the know, there is a big difference.

Quite simply, and in rather basic terms, the best way to differentiate between the two is this: The Cavalier King Charles has a nose, the King Charles does not.

Obviously this is not literally the case; the King Charles has a snub nose, the same as a Pug or Bulldog, whereas a Cavalier King Charles has a distinct muzzle, which is about $1\frac{1}{2}$ inches (3.8 cm) in length.

There are other subtle differences. The King Charles is slightly smaller and lighter boned, and has more bulbous eyes than the Cavalier, but essentially they come from the same basic mould.

Town or country?

The Cavalier is a dog you can take anywhere and he will be equally at home in a country mansion or a city apartment as long as he has a cosy bed – or preferably a sofa – to call his own.

His exercise can be tailored depending on the owner's individual circumstances, but access to a safe, secure garden should be considered essential.

It is possible to keep a small dog in a home that has no garden, but you would need to be very conscientious, taking your Cavalier out at regular intervals so that his toileting needs are met.

Collecting Cavaliers

The Cavalier is a sociable little dog and enjoys the company of other dogs, particularly his own kind. This is a breed that is highly collectable, and Cavs are perfectly happy to live in mini packs, as long as the owner is clearly established as a leader they can respect.

Living with other animals

Although the Cavalier is bred from sporting spaniels, he does not have a strong hunting instinct. This is probably because dogs have been selectively bred, over many generations, to be companions rather than working dogs.

This means that the Cavalier does not have a great desire to chase, so he will live in harmony with the family cat, as long as interactions are supervised from an early stage.

If you keep small animals, such as guinea pigs or hamsters, always err on the side of caution, and never allow a Cavalier unsupervised access. Accidents happen in a split second so it is always better to be safe than sorry.

Life expectancy

We are fortunate that the Cavalier is a relatively long-lived breed, and if you have a healthy dog that is fed the correct diet and kept at the correct weight, he should remain active until his early teens.

Tracing back in time

The Cavalier King Charles Spaniel gets his name from King Charles II (1630-1685) and his courtiers, but it is believed that most toy spaniels (and the ancestors of today's Cavalier) have their origins in the Far East from as far back as the 12th and 13th centuries.

Different types of toy spaniel, that could have had an influence on the Cavalier breed, evolved all over Europe. But perhaps the one that was most like the present day Cavalier, is believed to have come from either Holland or France.

These toy spaniels were favoured by the aristocrats and wealthy of the day, and were especially valued as ladies' companions.

Facing page:
Toy Spaniels were
popular in the royal
courts of Europe.

They have always had a strong connection with royalty; Mary Queen of Scots (1542-1587) held them in high regard and she is thought to have brought several dogs to Britain from France. When she was executed, a small, black and white spaniel was found hiding amongst her skirts.

It was during the reign of Charles II that the spaniels really came to the fore. No public buildings were off limits to the king's spaniels and he insisted they accompanied him everywhere – even on state occasions.

The diarist, Samuel Pepys, noted: "All I observed, there was the silliness of the King playing with his dog, all the while not minding the business."

William III came to the throne in 1689, and during his reign toy spaniels were usurped in popularity by Pugs he brought over from the Netherlands. However, they were restored to favour largely due to John Churchill, 1st Duke of Marlborough.

Not only was he a great soldier, he was also a keen dog breeder. He bred a strain of small chestnut and white spaniels, who were keen to retrieve, but equally content to be lapdogs for the ladies in court.

One of Churchill's greatest military successes was the Battle of Blenheim, 1704, which gives rise to one of the most famous stories of the Cavalier. It is said that while he was waging war in Germany, his wife, Sarah, sat at home anxiously waiting for news of her husband.

At the time she was nursing on her lap one of his heavily pregnant spaniels for comfort. In her nervous state she kept pressing her thumb down on top of the dog's head, and when the puppies were born each had a mark on its head, shaped like a thumb print.

Thus the 'lozenge', as we know it, had arrived, and it remains a much sought-after breed feature in Cavaliers to this day.

On his triumphant return, Queen Anne granted Churchill the title of Duke of Marlborough and gave him a large estate and grand palace in Oxfordshire, which became known as Blenheim Palace after his great victory. The spaniels, bred by Churchill, also adopted the name and were known as Blenheim spaniels.

Another famous royal to be associated with this type of toy spaniel was the young Queen Victoria. She was devoted to her small tri-color spaniel called Dash, and it is said that although she was very taken with the young Prince Albert, it was his warm behavior towards Dash that determined her attachment.

Facing page:
The lozenge mark on
the back of the head is
a sought-after feature
in Blenheim Cavaliers.

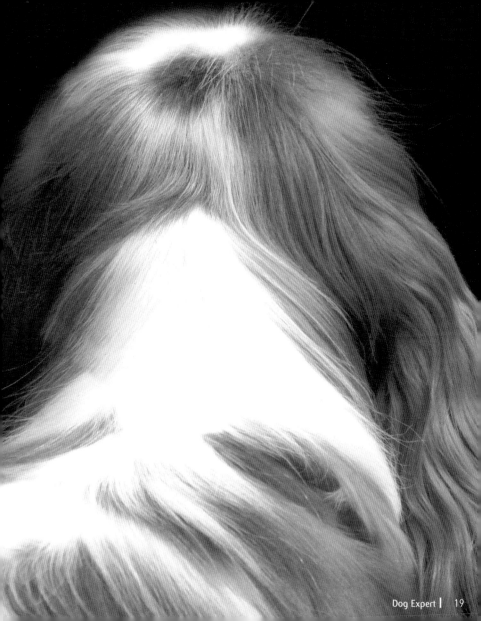

Developing the breed

It was during Queen Victoria's reign that the first organized dog shows were staged in the UK and this led to the formal recognition of many different breeds.

American challenge

Breeders of the day started to favour the shorter nosed, more dome skulled type of Blenheim spaniel and, thus, the early type of King Charles was seen. The longer nosed type of toy spaniel was becoming less and less prevalent, and it was not until the early 20th century that we hear of them again.

In the early 1920s an American gentleman and dog fancier by the name of Roswell Eldridge travelled to England and visited Crufts dog show. He was most disappointed not to find any of the longer nosed type of toy spaniel that he so admired – not only at Crufts but, it seemed, in all of the country. So he challenged

the King Charles Spaniel breeders of the day to produce:

Blenheim Spaniels of the Old Type, as shown in pictures of Charles II's time, long face, no stop, flat skull, not inclined to be domed with spot in centre of skull.

First prizes of £25 in Class 947 and 948 are given by Roswell Eldridge Esq., of New York, USA. Prizes go to nearest to type required.

The first classes were to be held at Crufts between 1926 and 1929. At first most breeders were not interested; they had spent too many years breeding the longer noses out. The first year there were only a few entries, but interest soon grew and a small band of determined breeders took up the gauntlet.

In 1928 a Blenheim spaniel called Ann's Son was awarded the £25 first prize. He was then used as the living specimen for the Breed Standard, the written blueprint for the breed, which remains practically unchanged. Sadly, Roswell Eldridge died a month before he was due to travel over to Crufts, so never saw the results of his challenge prizes.

Although Ann's Son does not look much like the Cavaliers of today, he was just what the breeders of yesteryear were looking for. He won the Eldridge prize three years running from 1928 to 1930, then came out again after six years in retirement to win again in 1936 as a sprightly nine-year-old.

A challenge was issued to find a Blenheim spaniel of the old type.

Breed recognition

By this stage spaniel breeders really had the bit between their teeth. A band of dedicated women was led by a very determined Mrs Amice Hewitt-Pitt, a well-known breeder of Chow Chows, and the Cavalier King Charles Spaniel Club was formed. The name 'Cavalier' was used to differentiate between the two types and was chosen to honour the famous painting by Landseer, The Cavalier's Pets, which so resembled the old type of toy spaniel that the intrepid band were trying to revive.

Progress was somewhat slow, as the Kennel Club refused to recognise this new breed and separate

them from their short-faced cousins. Thus the breed
garnered little interest, as at the time there was no
real financial reward for all the hard work involved.
But the pioneers kept slogging away and managed
to secure more guaranteed classes at shows, so that
eventually people realized that this 'new' little dog
was here to stay.

In 1945, the Kennel Club finally granted separate
recognition to the breed and the first set of
Challenge Certificates was awarded the following
year. The first Cavalier to attain his Champion's
crown in 1948, was fittingly owned by Mrs Amice
Pitt's daughter, Jane, and was named Daywell Roger.

Top honours

The breed continued to grow in popularity, and in 1963 Cavaliers won their first Crufts accolade when a Blenheim bitch won the Toy Group. Just 10 years later, a young Blenheim dog called Alansmere Aquarius was awarded Best In Show and named Crufts Supreme Champion.

This success catapulted the breed into the public domain and it quickly became the very popular breed that we know and love today.

Going global

The Cavalier King Charles Spaniel is now bred worldwide, with many breeders producing top-class dogs, particularly in Scandinavia.

The breed's history in the USA has been relatively short. The first recorded Cavalier to arrive in the US from England was Robrull Veren who was exported by Vera Rennie in the late 1940s and became the property of Mrs Harold Whitman of Bedford, New York.

British breeder Barbara Keswick sent a number of good-quality dogs to Elizabeth Spalding of Maine. She won Best in Show at the inaugural American Club Show with Pargeter Lotus of Kilspindle.

Miss Spalding was also instrumental in founding the Cavalier King Charles Club, which is still in existence. This was followed by the formation of the American Cavalier King Charles Spaniel Club in 1994, which worked towards American kennel Club recognition. This finally came in 1997.

The Cavalier is one of the more recent breeds to be recognized by the American Kennel Club.

What should a Cavalier look like?

All pedigree dogs have their own Breed Standard, which is a written description of the ideal specimen. It is a picture in words of what a particular breed should look like in terms of conformation, temperament and breed characteristics.

The Breed Standard is the 'bible' for breeders who try to produce dogs that adhere as closely as possible to its stipulations. It is also used by judges in the show ring who award places to the dogs that most closely fit the written blueprint.

The Breed Standard is, therefore, a document of great significance, as it has a profound effect on the way dogs are bred from generation to generation.

Breed Standards vary slightly depending on the national Kennel Club, but the differences are relatively minor.

General appearance

The Cavalier is an active, graceful dog that appears well balanced and in proportion. For a Toy breed, he has a surprisingly sporty appearance. Bred as a sweet-natured companion, the Cavalier's gentle expression is a hallmark of the breed.

Temperament

The Cavalier is described as "gay" which typifies the breed's happy attitude to life. This is a dog that is friendly with everyone he meets, showing no fear or nervousness, and most of all, no aggression.

Head and skull

It is the Cavalier's head, with his enchanting expression, that makes the breed. The skull should be almost flat between the ears, and the length from the base of the stop to the tip of the nose should be about $1^{1}/_{2}$ in (3.8 cm). The nose should be black, with well-developed nostrils, and there should be cushioning below the eyes.

Points of anatomy

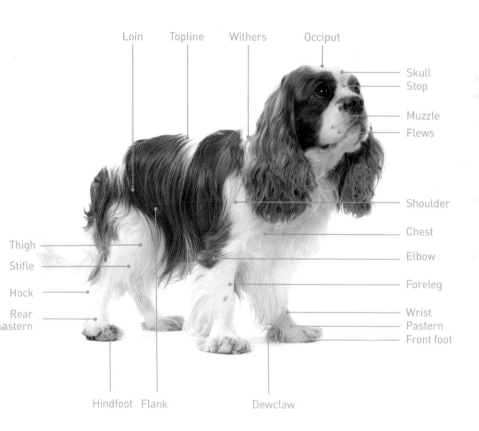

Loin · Topline · Withers · Occiput

Skull
Stop
Muzzle
Flews

Shoulder

Chest

Thigh
Stifle
Hock
Rear
pastern

Elbow

Foreleg

Wrist
Pastern
Front foot

Hindfoot · Flank · Dewclaw

Eyes

The dark brown eyes are large and round, and spaced well apart. They have a melting expression, which no Cavalier owner can resist!

Ears

These are set on high and are long and well feathered, framing the face.

Mouth

The jaws should be strong and the teeth should meet in a scissor bite, where the teeth on the upper jaw closely overlap the teeth on the lower jaw.

Body

The neck is slightly arched, flowing down to the shoulders, which are well laid back. The chest is moderate, and the front legs should be straight with the elbows close to the sides. The Cavalier is a short-coupled dog, which refers to the length between the last rib and the hip bone; the topline is level. The hindquarters are moderately muscled and moderately boned, with well-turned stifles.

Feet

The feet are rounded and well cushioned. Hair growing between the pads can be trimmed, but

trimming the hair around the feet is not allowed in the show ring.

Tail

The length of the tail should be in balance with the body to enhance his well-balanced appearance. The Standard says the tail should be carried "happily", although it should not go much above the level of the back. The happy, wagging tail is a characteristic of the breed, and one of his most endearing features.

Colors

The Cavalier comes in four colors
(pictured left to right on the opposite page):

Ruby: all over rich red.

Tri-color: mainly black and white makings with tan accents on the face, ears, and underside of tail.

Black and Tan: predominantly black with tan accents in the face, legs and feet, and underside of tail.

Blenheim: chestnut brown marking on pearly white background. The lozenge mark, between the ears, is a unique characteristic of the breed.

Coat

The Cavalier's long, silky coat should be gleaming with good health. A slight wave is allowed, but it

should not curl. Cavaliers have abundant feathering and this is never trimmed.

Movement

It is said that if a dog is put together, he will move correctly, which is why movement or 'gait', as it is termed, is always watched closely by judges in the show ring. Typically, the Cavalier should be free moving, yet elegant, showing plenty of drive from behind. The front legs and the hind legs move in parallel when viewed from behind.

Weight and size

The weight stipulated is between 12 and 18 lb (5.4-8.2 kg) which allows a wide range, even bearing in mind that males are slightly bigger than females. The Standard asks for "a small well-balanced dog within these weights". In reality, most show dogs tend to be at the upper end of the range.

The Breed Standard in the UK does not give measurements for height, but the American Standard states that dogs should be 12-13 in (30-32 cm) at the withers, which is the highest point of the shoulder.

Summing up

The dream is to produce the perfect dog that is identical to the description laid out in the Breed Standard. Of course, this is an impossibility, as every dog will have a flaw, no matter how unimportant. It is also important to bear in mind that the Breed Standard is open to individual interpretation, so one judge's idea of perfection may be quite different from another's.

However, the priority for judges and breeders alike is to produce sound, healthy dogs, without exaggeration, which are typical of the breed.

What do you want from your Cavalier?

For many, the Cavalier King Charles Spaniel is the breed that has it all. Beautiful to look at, loving and devoted, what more could you ask? However, it is important to make sure that your expectations match the reality before taking the plunge into Cavalier ownership.

Companion dog

If you are looking for a companion, look no further! The Cavalier was bred specifically to be a lapdog, and this is the role he excels at. Cavaliers love people and want nothing more than to spend every minute of the day with their beloved owners.

Show dog

Do you have ambitions to exhibit your Cavalier in the show ring? This is not as easy as it sounds; it is a pastime that demands hard work and dedication – plus a reasonable amount of money, as travelling to shows and entry fees are not cheap. However, the most important aspect of showing is to get the right dog.

There is no percentage in going to a breeder and hoping you will get a show quality puppy when you say you are looking for a pet. This is unfair on the breeder, and will only result in disappointment. You must be completely transparent so the breeder knows you are looking for a puppy with show potential, and will be able to help you with your choice.

Bear in mind that a puppy can only have 'show potential'. The breeder, and anyone else who is experienced in the breed, can evaluate the puppy, weighing up his strengths and weaknesses in relation to how closely he conforms to the Breed Standard. However, puppies go through many different stages as they develop, and the pup with great promise may not make the grade.

If this happens, you must be prepared to love your Cavalier for the wonderful dog he is, and maybe look elsewhere for a show dog.

Other ambitions

The Cavalier is one of the most versatile of the toy breeds, and can be trained to a reasonable level in Obedience. Many owners who enjoy competing have opted for Agility, which the Cavalier thoroughly enjoys.

If you want to do something more with your Cavalier, another option is to train him for therapy work. This involves working on basic obedience and good manners so your Cavalier is registered to visit hospitals, schools and residential homes. The Cavalier is a handy size, and his gentle, affectionate temperament makes him an ideal candidate.

What does your Cavalier want from you?

The Cavalier is an adaptable dog and will do his utmost to fit in with your lifestyle. However, like all living creatures, he has his own special needs.

Companionship

We have highlighted the Cavalier's exceptional qualities as a companion dog. This is one of the attractions of owning the breed, but it also brings responsibilities. The Cavalier was bred to be with people, and this is his *raison d'être*. If he is excluded from family activities, or left for long periods on his own, he will be miserable.

Obviously, you can make arrangements for dog-sitters to help out, or there are other options such as day care, but these can be costly. If you do

not have the time to devote to a Cavalier, you should maybe wait until your circumstances change.

Leadership

The Cavalier is only a small dog, but this does not mean that you can neglect his training. In order to fit in with your family, a Cavalier must have a leader he respects.

The Cavalier is an integral member of the family, but he must live within the boundaries that you set down. You are the decision-maker and your Cavalier must accept this without argument.

Right from the start, teach your Cavalier what is acceptable behavior and reward him when he co-operates. Be 100 per cent consistent so your Cavalier understands what is expected of him at all times. In this way, your Cavalier will accept his place in the family, and will learn that abiding by your rules brings its own rewards.

Exercising mind and body

The Cavalier does not need a huge amount of exercise – he will be more than happy with a daily routine of a couple of 20 minute outings, plus time out in the garden.

However, it is important to bear in mind that an intelligent dog such as the Cavalier needs more than physical exercise. He also requires mental stimulation.

This can come in a variety of forms:

- You can take your Cavalier on different walks so he has the opportunity to investigate new sights and smells

- You can play retrieve games, or run through some basic obedience exercises.

- Some owners enjoy teaching tricks, and the Cavalier certainly enjoys the opportunity to show off his talents!

Basically, it does not matter what you do, as long as you give your dog something to occupy his active mind. A Cavalier that has a busy, stimulating life will be far easier to live with than a dog that is bored and frustrated.

Extra considerations

Now you have chosen the Cavalier as the breed to suit your lifestyle, you need to narrow your choice so that you know exactly what you are looking for. Choosing the right Cavalier makes a big difference to how easily your dog will adapt to his new home.

Male or female?

The first thing to decide is whether you would prefer to have a male or a female. So let us weigh up the pros and cons. There are many old wives' tales associated with both sexes, so it is worth seeing if any truth lies behind the myths.

Males have the propensity for going off looking for bitches in season.

Very few males are so sexually charged that they will, at every opportunity, escape to go searching for bitches.

Males 'cock' their legs in the house.

Yes, some males might be more prone to marking their territory in the house, but this is learnt behavior and if it is not allowed from the very beginning it should not become a problem.

Males show sexual behavior mounting cushions, chair legs and even children.

This should be regarded more as a dominance driven activity than a sexual one. Again, this can be trained out of a male purely by establishing yourself as the pack leader. If this fails, neutering will usually resolve the problem.

Neutering (castrating) a male is recommended as it has health benefits, such as avoiding the risk of testicular cancer, as well as inhibiting more hormone-driven behavior. However, if you delay neutering and allow 'male' behavior to become established, it will not cease after neutering.

Females are more aloof.

A female Cavalier can be a little bit 'diva-ish', preferring to do things on her terms. Her attitude is: "if you want to admire me, I look better sitting on this pink cushion on this comfy chair than up close and personal".

I have experienced different levels of affection with both males and females but, generally, I do find the boys are more affectionate and willing to please – but every dog owner will tell you something different.

Females have two seasons a year and are very unclean during this time.

Yes, bitches that are not neutered have seasons – that is a fact. This is when the vulva swells and the female starts to bleed from it. Some different pedigree lines have longer gaps between the seasons, but the norm is for a bitch to come into season every six months, from the age of around six months.

Each season will last for anything up to four weeks, but averages around 21 days. Some bitches are by nature, not very clean – and, believe me, a bitch in season can really pong! During the three weeks the bitch is in season, she will be very attractive to male dogs and she should be confined to barracks during this time so as not to cause trouble among the neighboring dog population.

With all this in mind, you then have to ask whether this is something that you would be able to deal with. Obviously the solution to this is having your bitch neutered (spayed), which is an option to discuss with your vet.

There are many health benefits associated with spaying, such as avoiding the risk of mammary tumors and pyometra, which is a life-threatening condition. In most cases, vets recommend spaying at the midway point between the first and second season.

When it comes to choosing a male or a female Cavalier, only you can decide which would be best for you and your circumstances, but do listen to people who have experience of both sexes.

Color

The next step is to decide which color – and we are lucky in this breed that there are four beautiful colors to choose from.

Blenheim (chestnut and white) is the most popular, closely followed by tri-color, with the black and tan and ruby bringing up the rear. I think the reason the whole colors are not as popular as the parti-colors is simply because, for a long time, the public just did not know they existed. In the last few decades, as more whole colors have had success in the show ring, more have been bred. Therefore more have been seen, increasing the demand for them.

I was lucky enough to win Best of Breed at Crufts in 1995 with a ruby dog of mine called Kevin. He was, and still is, the only ruby male to have won this accolade in the breed's history. He was caught by the TV cameras for about 20 seconds and the interest in rubies shot up by a huge margin.

There is no difference, temperament wise, in the four colors, nor in coat texture, thickness or length.

More than one?

Cavalier puppies are irresistible, and it can be tempting to take home two puppies from the same litter, thinking they will be company for each other. They will be – but you will soon come to regret your decision.

The puppies will bond so closely with each other, they may fail to relate to you. They will also be far harder to train, unless you are very disciplined and can give them lots of individual attention.

If you want two Cavaliers, the best plan is to wait until your first is about 18 months old before acquiring a second.

An older dog

Occasionally, a breeder may have an older dog that needs a home – and if you want to miss out the puppy stage this could be an ideal solution.

It could be that the puppy has been 'run on' as a potential show dog but has failed to make the grade. A minor fault, such as incorrect tail carriage, will mar a show career, but the dog will still make a wonderful companion.

The other option is to take on a rescued dog. These can be found at all-breed rescue centres, and also through breed clubs which run their own rehoming schemes. These dogs have often been put up for rehoming through no fault of their own – family break up, a new job, or the arrival of a new baby are the most common reasons.

If you want to go down this route, try to find out as much about the dog in question as possible. You need to find out what his previous home was like – whether there were children, other dogs or cats – to see if he is likely to fit in with your lifestyle.

Remember, an older dog will take time to adjust, so you will need to be patient for the first few months as he settles into his new home.

Sourcing
a puppy

It is very easy to go on the Internet and find hundreds of sites with puppies of all breeds for sale.

The majority of these websites are set up and supplied by brokers. In other words, the puppies are bred off site, and then shipped in to be offered for sale.

The chances are that any puppies supplied this way will have started life in what is termed as a puppy mill or puppy farm, where litters are produced purely for profit, with no consideration given to health, temperament or socialization.

Puppy farms

These are places where dogs are farmed, just like livestock, but with considerably less care and attention. Puppies may cost half what you might pay a reputable breeder. But the chances are that the 'bargain' puppy will cost you many times over in vet fees. You may also face the heartbreak of dealing with a sick dog, who may well develop major behavioral problems associated with poor breeding and lack of socialization.

The right way

The best starting place is national Kennel Club
websites – both the American Kennel Club, and the
Kennel Club in the UK have excellent sites which
give you lots of information about Cavaliers (and
other breeds) and how best to choose a puppy.

There are registers of puppies for sale, and if you opt for an accredited breeder – known as a breeder of merit in the US, and an assured breeder in the UK – you will know that a code of ethics has been adhered to.

You can also find details of breed clubs, and this is an excellent route to sourcing a healthy puppy from a responsible breeder. Again, club members will usually have followed a code of ethics, ensuring that breeding stock and puppies have been produced to the highest standards.

Health issues

The top priority is to find a typical Cavalier puppy that is healthy. Like all breeds, the Cavalier is affected by a number of inherited health problems (see page 180), so you need to make sure that the breeder has carried out all the necessary health clearances.

It should be made clear that not all breed lines are affected. However, even if the parents are thought to be free of a problem, it may be that they are carrying a mild form, which may then show in a severe fashion amongst the offspring. It is, therefore, a wise precaution to ask the breeder what conditions the parents have been tested for, and find out as much as possible about puppies produced from these lines.

Golden rules

When you make contact with a breeder bear in mind the following guidelines to ensure you will be getting a healthy, well-bred puppy:

- Make sure you see the puppy with his mother. Some people advise seeing the father also, but in reality, very often the father usually belongs to another breeder and is not living on site.

- Depending on the age you go to see the pup, he should still be with his littermates. Ask to see the other puppies in the litter. Look where they are kept and how they play with each other.

- Ask if you can see other dogs on the premises, especially if they are related to the puppies. See how they interact with one another and check out overall well-being and friendliness.

- Find out when the puppies are allowed to go to their new homes. Responsible breeders will not let puppies go until they are at eight weeks old; some will even keep them longer than this.

- Ask if the puppies have been vet checked. Ideally, this should happen before the puppies go to their new homes, otherwise the sale should be dependent on a vet check within 48 hours of purchase.

Puppy
watching

When you find a litter, bred by a responsible breeder, you will be desperate to go and view the puppies. However, it is better to wait until they are about four weeks of age.

In the first few weeks, the puppies are pretty much like beached whales – just lying there waiting for the 'milk-bar' to arrive, have a good feed and then back to sleep. It is therefore better to wait until they are more active, and the mother will also be more relaxed and welcoming when her puppies are a little older.

If you do go to see a litter at this age, be careful not to set your heart on a particular pup. It is fairly unusual to be able to choose your puppy from a litter, as the breeder will probably be waiting to decide which one they want to keep. You could intimate which one you like the look of, but it is better not to set yourself up for disappointment.

What to look for

There are the obvious things to be aware of when looking at a litter of puppies. Make a mental note of the ones that seem more outgoing, running forward to greet you, whilst some of the others might hang back a little more. But do be aware that the next time you visit, the chances are that the same puppy who seemed a bit shy and retiring, may be all over you.

I have had many a puppy, over the years, who, when faced with a prospective buyer, steadfastly refused to do anything but sit and look cute in the whelping box while his littermates were running riot. Then on the next visit, the sedate pup would be racing round like a whirlwind, hell bent on beating his brothers and sisters up in a very thuggish manner!

Do not be put off if the puppy you are offered is a bit smaller than his littermates. This is not necessarily the runt of the litter. There will always be a smallest puppy born in a litter, and because he is smaller, he will not put on as much weight, or at the same rate, as his littermates. This does not mean that he will not make normal size when fully grown or be more predisposed to health problems.

When you go to look at a prospective litter, I believe that instinct counts for a lot. Sometimes you just get a feeling that all is not well. If this is the case, be brave and sensible and turn down the puppy you have been offered. It is far better to be cautious than to repent at leisure.

A Cavalier friendly home

So you have found your puppy! The next step is to get everything ready for his arrival, ensuring that your home is safe and you have all the necessary equipment. These preparations apply to a new puppy but, in reality, they are the means of creating an environment that is safe and secure for your Cavalier throughout his life.

Safety in the home

An inquisitive Cavalier puppy will want to explore his new home so it is important that you make sure the environment is safe. It helps if you see things from your puppy's perspective, and then you can restrict his access or move things out of his reach.

There are many potential dangers for a puppy in the home, purely because he investigates everything with his mouth. These include trailing electric wires, cupboards with cleaners and detergents which could be toxic, children's toys left around, shoes, slippers, house plants – the list is endless.

You and your family need to get into the habit of keeping valuables – and anything else that is chewable – out of the puppy's way.

You may well find that a baby-gate, restricting access to the upstairs, or any other room, will make life easier.

In the garden

Next you need to thoroughly check your garden. It needs to be 100 per cent safe and secure, as a curious puppy has no perception of danger.

The Cavalier is not a great escaper, but you should check fencing and hedges, making sure there are no puppy-size gaps. Gates leading out of the garden should have secure fastenings; if visitors use a gate, you may need to put up a 'Please Close The Gate' notice.

Garden ponds are a potential hazard; tragically I have heard of puppies drowning in small ponds and pools, mainly because they have exhausted

Facing page:
The inquisitive Cavalier will explore every nook and cranny of your garden.

themselves trying to get out. So, if you do have a water feature in your garden, you might think about making a cover for it, or maybe temporarily fencing it off, until the puppy has grown enough in size to eliminate the worry.

Next, look at what plants you have. There are many plants that are actually highly poisonous to dogs – you can find a full list on the internet (see page 191). I am not suggesting you should go round yanking all these plants out, but just be aware they are there. A puppy's favorite pastime is to chew anything he can get his teeth into!

Buying equipment

There are some essential items of equipment you will need for your Cavalier. If you choose wisely, much of it will last for many years to come.

Indoor crate

I consider that having a crate for your new puppy is a must; I cannot stress enough the usefulness of having one. A crate can be used to keep your puppy safe and secure when you have to go out, and it provides a cosy den at night. There are times in the day when you cannot supervise your puppy, or you may have visitors who don't like dogs – again, the crate provides the solution.

You can also use a crate in the car, allowing your Cavalier to travel in safety, and you can take it with you if you are staying away from home.

It is important to buy a crate that is big enough for an adult Cavalier, as many dogs will use them throughout their lives. The ideal size of crate is 24 in long x 18 in wide x 18 in high (60 cm x 45 cm x 45 cm).

You will also need to consider where you are going to locate the crate. The kitchen is usually the most suitable place as this is the hub of the household. Try to find a snug corner where the puppy can rest when he wants to, but where he can also see what is going on around him, and still be with the family.

Beds and bedding

The best type of bedding is a synthetic fleece, known in the UK as Vetbed. It can be used in both the crate and in any other bed you might have for your puppy. It has an absorbent backing and is especially useful when your puppy is learning the basics of toilet training. If he should make a mistake, urine will soak straight through leaving a dry surface for your puppy to lie on.

If you have purchased a crate, you may not feel the need for an extra bed, but if you decide to get one I would recommend a plastic oval or round bed that will accommodate your puppy when he is fully grown.

Collars and leads

Remember, the type of collar and lead you buy for the early days will be quite different to the one the puppy will be wearing when he is fully-grown.

To begin with, I would recommend a soft, nylon collar with a clip fastening rather than a buckle fastening for your young puppy to wear as an everyday collar.

I would also use this type of collar as his first 'walking' collar, although I would probably get a slightly more substantial one. Once your Cavalier is fully-grown, you can have fun choosing what colors and patterns you prefer.

You can usually buy a lead to match the collar you have decided on, or it may be worth investing in a leather lead as it is going to take some wear and tear over the years.

A couple of things to bear in mind when buying your puppy's lead: make sure the clip on the lead is not too big, or it will bang into his neck and face. Also ensure the lead is not too long, or it will be difficult to handle.

Bowls

The range of bowls available is wide– from cheap, but colorful plastic to ceramic and stainless steel. Plastic bowls have a tendency to split, and if they are chewed bacteria can get into the chew marks. They do not wear well, and will need replacing fairly regularly.

Although ceramic bowls are more hygienic and easier to keep clean, they are breakable, so I use stainless steel.

They are hygienic, easy to clean, and they are virtually indestructible. They come in various sizes and weights.

You can also buy 'spaniel' bowls which are good for keeping the ears out of the food and water when a dog is eating or drinking, the theory being that the ears will hang down outside the bowl.

Grooming equipment

The Cavalier is a long-coated breed, and needs regular grooming. You will need:

- A slicker brush, which is a rubber pad covered in metal teeth attached to a plastic handle. This brush is ideal to use on the longer feathering, as it will gently remove any small knots.

- A soft bristle brush to use on the body coat.

- A medium toothed comb is a must. This is used as a follow through after brushing to get any extra dead hair out that has not been removed by either the slicker or bristle brushes, and to remove any small knots. A double-ended comb is ideal, with fine teeth at one end, and wide teeth the other.

- Guillotine nail clippers. They work exactly as they sound, and are by far the easiest and kindest nail clippers to use.

Toys

The Cavalier loves nothing more than to play, on his own or with company. Most types of manufactured dog toys are suitable, plus knotted old socks, rubber balls and rope tugs.

Bones and chews

There are only two types of bones or chews I would recommend for either a new puppy or an older dog. These are sterilised bones and sterilised cow hooves.

These are both really good for the teeth, and dogs seem to love them. As they are pre-cooked, there is no risk of the bones splintering. You can buy them filled with marrowbone, which my dogs find irresistible! However, hooves are their favorite treat and they will lie for hours crunching on them.

I would never give rawhide chews, as trouble may arise when the dog has been chewing on one for a while and it becomes soggy and starts to unravel. If the dog tries to swallow the chew, it can get stuck in his throat and choke him.

Food

Your breeder will have let you know what your puppy was eating and should provide a full diet sheet to guide you through the first six months of your puppy's feeding regime.

This should include how much they are eating per meal, how many meals per day, when to increase the amounts given per meal and when to reduce the meals per day. The breeder may provide you with some food when you go to collect your new puppy.

ID

Your Cavalier needs ID when he is out in public places. This can be in the form of a disc, engraved with your contact details, that can be attached to the collar. When your Cavalier is older, you can buy a collar embroidered with your contact details, which eliminates the danger of the disc becoming detached from the collar.

You may also wish to consider a permanent form of ID. Increasingly, breeders are getting puppies microchipped before they go to their new homes. A microchip is the size of a grain of rice. It is 'injected' under the skin, usually between the shoulder blades.

Each chip has its own unique identification number, which is then registered on a national database with your name and details, so that if ever your dog is lost, he can be taken to any vet or rescue centre where he is scanned and then you are contacted.

If your puppy has not been microchipped, you can ask your vet to do it.

Another way to ID your dog is by tattooing. This is usually done at about six weeks, and the whole litter is done at the same time. A number is stamped on the inside of the ear, and sprayed with permanent ink. As the puppy grows, so does the tattoo. Again, the number is registered, along with all your details, on a national database. It is also possible to have an older dog tattooed.

Finding a vet

Before your puppy arrives home, you should find and register yourself with a vet. You need to find someone you can build up a good rapport with and have complete faith in. Word of mouth is really the best recommendation.

When you contact a veterinary practice, find out the following:

- Does the surgery run an appointment system?

- What are the arrangements for emergency, out of hours cover?

- Do any of the vets in the practice have experience treating Cavaliers?

- What facilities are available at the practice?

If you are buying your puppy locally, ask your breeder which vet they use. A breeder will have more experience with vets than the average pet owner, and it may be prudent to use the same practice, especially if the puppy has already been checked by them. You will need to provide all your new puppy's details when you register – breed, date of birth, gender and color.

Settling in

At last it is time for your puppy to come to his new home. This is an exciting time, but remember that it can be overwhelming for the little one, no matter how confident he is.

For the first few days, a puppy needs to find his bearings and investigate his new surroundings. Therefore you should resist the temptation of inviting friends and family to come and see him. It is enough that he gets used to his own home and becomes familiar with the people he is going to be living with.

If you have children, try to keep them as calm as possible, and make sure they are sitting on the floor when they play with the puppy. A pup can be very wriggly, so if everyone is a floor level, you eliminate the risk of an accident.

After exploring his new home and meeting his new family, your puppy will be quite tired, so pop him away in his crate to recharge his batteries. The sooner he starts getting used to his crate the better. If he has short spells in there to begin with, he will

learn that it is a cosy den where he can rest in peace.

Offer him food as laid out in the diet sheet given to you by his breeder, but do not be too concerned if he does not show much enthusiasm – this is not unusual. It is more than likely that he will not eat on the first day as there is simply too much going on in his new world.

The resident dog

If you already have a dog at home, it is important that relations with the new arrival get off to a good start. The best place to introduce them is in the garden, which is relatively neutral territory.

Allow the two dogs to meet, and try not to be over-protective of the puppy. It is very rare that an adult dog would harm a puppy as the pup will be using body language to show he is submissive, making sure that he is not perceived as a threat. It is far better to allow the two dogs to communicate – canine to canine – so they can work out their own relationship.

In the first few weeks, supervise mealtimes and play times, and make sure the puppy is crated overnight. In this way, the puppy and adult will get used to each other without any pressure and, in no time, they will be the best of friends.

The first night

The first day in a new home will be exhausting for your puppy and he will be more than ready for bed when you are. Go outside with him for a few minutes while he relieves himself, then bring him in and snuggle him down in his crate. Put one of his toys in with him. If you have a radio in the room, leave it on low for background noise.

This is the time when you will find a crate invaluable. Your puppy has come from being with his littermates to a strange house and is then left, alone, in a large, dark room. It is in situations like this that a puppy can become stressed, noisy or destructive. If he is in a crate, you can be confident that he cannot come to any harm.

Once your puppy is in his crate, turn out the light and close the door. It is more than likely that he will kick up a fuss and bark, but do not go down to him. If you do, you will be making a rod for your own back. This commotion will probably last no more than half an hour before he realizes all his efforts are wasted, so he may as well give up and go to sleep. The rule of thumb is: the puppy must fit in with you, not you with him.

The next morning

The next morning, your puppy will be encouraging you to rise and shine early on, but don't rush to him. He has survived the night, so he can wait another few minutes. Puppies are very quick to learn at this age – both good manners and bad – and it won't take him long to work out that crying and yapping will get him what he wants...attention. So it is very important that he learns that he can, indeed, have all the attention he desires – but in your time not his.

House
training

One of the first things you will need to tackle is house training. In reality, this is not the ordeal you may be dreading. If you work hard in the first weeks, your puppy will soon learn what is required.

The best plan is to allocate a toileting area in your garden and take your puppy to this spot every time he needs to relieve himself. He will quickly build up an association and will know why you have brought him out to the garden.

Establish a routine and make sure you take your puppy out at the following times:

- First thing in the morning

- After mealtimes

- On waking from a sleep

- Following a play session

- Last thing at night

A puppy should be taken out to relieve himself every two hours as an absolute minimum. If you can manage an hourly trip out, so much the better. The more often your puppy gets it 'right', the quicker he will learn to be clean in the house.

If you do go outside with him and he starts jumping up at you and not concentrating on the job in hand, turn your back and ignore him. You could think of a word to use, such as "toilet" or "busy" which will trigger the correct response. You can then give him lots of praise and maybe have a quick game with him, before heading back to the house.

Keep an eye on your puppy when he is in the house, and if he starts circling, or looking as though he is searching for something, you can guarantee that he is about to toilet. Quickly pop him outside again and once he has performed bring him back in and lavish him with praise.

It becomes tricky when the weather is not good. But your puppy will still need to relieve himself, so you have to harden your heart. Go outside with him, as you normally would, encourage him and then if he performs, bring him straight back in and, again, shower him with praise. If he won't go and just sits looking pathetic, bring him back in for a while, watch him like a hawk and as soon as he starts doing his searching behavior again put him straight back out.

Keep repeating this until you eventually get a result. He will soon learn that the quicker he performs, the less time he has to spend in the rain.

When accidents happen

No matter how vigilant you are, there are bound to be accidents. If you witness the accident, take your puppy outside immediately, and give him lots of praise if he finishes his business out there.

If you are not there when he has an accident, do not scold him when you finally do see what has happened. He will not remember what he has done and will not understand why his owner is so cross.

Make sure you use a deodorizer after you clean up so your pup is not tempted to use the same spot again.

Choosing
a diet

Providing a well-balanced diet is an essential part of caring for your Cavalier King Charles Spaniel. But what is the best food to choose and how do you decide on a feeding regime?

Some things to take into consideration when deciding are:

- Ease of use

- Cost

- Storage

- Health benefits

Let us first concentrate on the advantages and disadvantages of raw or canned meat and mixer.

Pros

- It is highly palatable and most dogs love raw, cooked or canned meat.

- Mixer is good for providing roughage – keeping the teeth clean and bulking out the meat

Cons

- Canned meat is not cheap, and although raw meat is cheaper, it is usually sold in blocks which are frozen, so you have to remember to get them out of the freezer the night before.

- With any meat – raw or canned – there is an element of risk with regard to harbouring bacteria. Raw meat also has a much shorter shelf life.

- There is very little nutritional value in most canned meat – often it is around 75 per cent water.

- There is also limited nutritional value in raw meat. Yes, dogs in the wild would be eating it. But they would also be eating the bones, hair and organs that would supply the vitamins and minerals.

- Most mixers are wheat gluten based, and it has become apparent that some dogs have an intolerance.

Now let us look at complete food:

Pros

- Complete food is exactly what it says. It is a perfectly balanced diet, containing the correct amount of fat, protein, vitamins and minerals needed, to keep a dog in the best condition possible.

- It is easy to store and has a long shelf life.

- It can be bought in larger amounts which often works out more economical in the long term.

- It is always in hard kibble form which is good for keeping the teeth clean.

Below: It is important to find a diet that suits your own Cavalier.

- There is a wide range available, some adapted to different life stages, such as puppy, adult maintenance and senior.

Cons

- Your dog might not like it. It is the only thing that I can say against complete diets, and even that is very unusual.

Regardless of the diet you choose, fresh drinking water must be freely available.

Feeding regimes

When your puppy arrives in his new home, he will probably be on four meals a day – breakfast, lunch, dinner and supper. To begin with it is important to stick with the food your breeder recommends, as a sudden change in diet may lead to digestive upset.

I would advise you to feed your puppy in his crate, so that he is confined and has to concentrate on the job in hand. It also helps to build up a good association with the crate. Give him 10 to 15 minutes – no more – to clear the bowl. If he has not done so, just take it away and let him out.

Do not, under any circumstances, be tempted to add treats to his food to tempt him to eat. This is quite simply the worst thing you can do. If your puppy was eating perfectly well when he came to you, and taking into account his 24-hour settling in period, there is absolutely no reason why he should not carry on eating.

As soon as you start to offer him little treats he will learn that you are a soft touch and he can wrap you around his little paw. If he is hungry enough he will eat – simple as that!

If, for any reason, you need to change the diet, do it gradually. Feed the normal diet, and then add in a little of the new food. Continue doing this day by day, and by the end of a week, you will have made the transition, hopefully, without upsetting your puppy's digestive system.

At around 12 weeks of age, you can cut down to three meals a day, then, at about 16-20 weeks, you might notice a little reluctance to eat creeping in again. Don't panic!

The chances are your puppy is starting to teethe, losing his baby teeth and growing his adult set. This can cause some pain and discomfort, so during this period, which usually lasts a few weeks, it might help to moisten the food with warm water.

Some people prefer to keep their adult dogs on two meals as they feel it is better to spread it rather than feeding it all in one go. Others like to feed their dogs just once a day. In reality, it makes no difference so feel free to choose whatever fits in with your everyday living.

You will need to adjust the quantity you are feeding as your puppy grows.

Ideal weight

Cavaliers have a knack of giving us 'the eye' when it comes to food, but you have to be firm. A dog that is the correct weight will be healthier and will live longer. In my view a Cavalier should be reasonably well covered but have a defined waistline.

If you give your dogs extra treats, such as when you are training him, you need to deduct the amount from his overall ration.

If your dog has a healthy diet, of the right proportions, but still seems hungry, you can add some vegetables – particularly cabbage, broccoli, and raw carrot. This adds bulk and makes him feel full, but without risking weight gain.

Caring
for your
Cavalier

The Cavalier is a relatively easy breed to look after, but it is best to get into a routine of providing regular care.

Puppy grooming

When you first get your puppy he will not require much in the way of coat care, but it is important that he gets used to being handled, so he accepts – and enjoys – being groomed when his adult coat comes through.

With a puppy, use a soft bristle brush, as anything else will be a little harsh on the coat. Start with the puppy on the floor. Gently restrain him and run the brush all over his body. He will probably think it is a great game and try and grab the brush from you. Gently discourage him and get him to stand still for five to ten minutes, continuing to brush him.

When you have done this praise him, maybe give him a treat and have a game with him so he can get rid of his pent up energy. This is all part of the learning curve. As he gets more and more used to being groomed and handled, you could try putting him up on a table, as long you are sure of his safety.

A puppy needs to get used to being handled.

Pick up each paw in turn.

Check the ears.

Part the lips and examine the teeth.

Adult grooming

As the coat develops and your Cavalier starts to grow feathering on his legs, tail, ears and undercarriage, you will need to introduce the slicker brush. This piece of equipment is vital to your grooming kit; It is the kindest and most efficient way of removing little knots.

When the coat is knot free, the brush will go through the coat 'slickly' (hence the name). There is no sound. But if there is a knot in the feather, even a tiny one, the brush will drag slightly every time it hits the snag and you can also hear when it does. As you brush through continually, the little wires on the brush break down the knot until eventually it is brushed out.

But use this brush with caution – because of the type of wires on it, if it is used with to much force, it can cause brush burn. This makes the dog's skin sore. Blood rushes to the surface and it will create a rash. So take the slicker brush through the ears, brushing upward first to get to the fine under hair, then downwards on the top hair.

Follow this through with a metal comb, paying particular attention to the back of the ear where the hair grows thickest. This is the area most prone to matting, especially because this is where dogs scratch at the ear the most.

Start by brushing through the coat.

Pay particular attention to the feathering.

You can use a spray to help you work through any tangles in the coat.

Once the coat is brushed you can go through it with a comb.

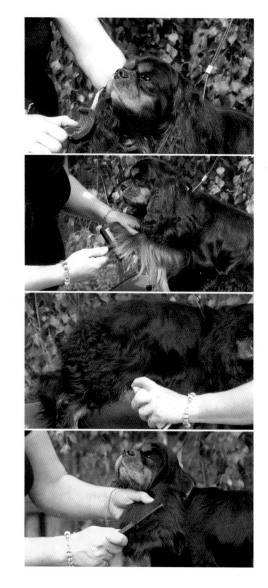

Once the ears are done, pick up the front leg. Run the slicker brush through the feathering and over the feet. When the foot furnishings grow, they can get nasty little knots between the toes, so it is a good idea to get him used to having his feet groomed as well.

Then pay attention to his undercarriage, his 'trousers' and finally his tail. When doing his trousers, make sure you get the brush right into the inside of the back leg. Again, this is a harbour for little knots and tags and, if left undetected, they can end up as great mats of knotted hair that may then have to be cut out. As you will imagine, it is quite a sensitive area, and most dogs will not appreciate too much brushing or pulling. Everywhere you have been with the slicker brush, follow through with the comb, just to remove any extra dead hair that might still be there.

To keep on top of the coat, I would recommend this be done once a week – more at times of the year when they are shedding, which is usually at the beginning of the summer and at the end of the autumn.

Bathing

A once a week grooming session will, hopefully, keep the coat in good condition and knot free, but your Cavalier will still get dirty so I recommend a bath every four to six weeks. Don't do it more often or you may wash out the natural oils, leaving the coat a little dry.

There is a wealth of different shampoos to choose from specifically for dogs, as well as conditioners and coat sprays, which are all designed to be gentle on the coat.

Step by step

- When you are bathing your Cavalier, remember to put a piece of cotton wool (cotton) in each of his ears. Make sure it is not too small or it may get pushed too far down the ear, but not too big so that it falls out. You just want to block the ear canal so no water goes down, which is tickly and irritating for the dog.

- Put your dog in the bath or shower. Get the water to the right temperature (about what you feel comfortable with on the back of your hand). Wet him through thoroughly, right down to the skin.

- Apply shampoo to the coat and lather it up. It really is the same as washing your own hair. Work the shampoo into a really good lather, giving the skin a good massage at the same time. This brings the blood to the surface, which nourishes the skin and coat.

- When you have shampooed him thoroughly, start to rinse. Again this is like doing your own hair. Keep rinsing until the water runs clear and until you hear the 'squeak' as you run your hand over the coat.

- Run you hands firmly all over his body to wring out any excess water – he will probably have a good old shake to help with this process.

- When you have wrung out as much water as you can by hand, give him a rub down with a towel, remembering to dry all the feathering and underneath.

- The best and quickest way to dry a dog is with a hairdryer. Because most dogs won't be particularly keen on the sound or feel of the dryer to begin with, the whole drying process might be a bit of a chore, but eventually your Cavalier will get used to it.

Do not hold the dryer too close to his body, and don't aim it at one spot directly. You could easily burn him by doing this. Try to wave the dryer up and down so the heat is dispersed more evenly. If he is sitting still, you can brush the coat in different directions as you are drying it. This will help to speed up the drying process and verify he is dry right through to the skin.

Routine care

While you are grooming your dog, use the opportunity for some other routine checks.

Teeth

You Cavalier's teeth should be clean and white, with no noticeable bad breath. If he is eating dry food, the act of crunching on the kibble will help to keep plaque and tartar at bay, as will chewing on bones and hooves. You can also get a special toothpaste, and brushing his teeth once a week will be beneficial.

Ears

As the Cavalier has 'drop' ears, there is greater chance he will suffer from ear problems. If you see your dog persistently scratching his ear or shaking his head vigorously, you can be fairly sure he has an ear problem, so a trip to the vet might be necessary.

It helps if you keep the ears clean and fresh. You can do this by to putting a dab of surgical spirit on to a pad of cotton wool, and gently wiping all round the inside of the ear and the opening of the ear canal. Do not put the surgical spirit directly into the ear, and only use it sparingly.

Eyes

The eyes should be clear, bright and sparkling. If necessary, wipe away debris using a moist cotton-wool (cotton) pad.

Nails

Keep a check on your Cavalier's nails to make sure they do not grow too long. Nails can be trimmed using the guillotine type of nail clippers, taking a sliver off at a time. Be careful not to cut into the quick – the blood vessel in the nails – as it will bleed, causing some discomfort to your dog. If this does happen, get some cotton wool (cotton) and hold it firmly on the end of the nail until the bleeding stops.

As you cut the nails, the quick will recede down the nail, so the more you do them, the further the quick will recede. Thus you will be able to keep the nails really short. Be aware that dogs generally do not like having their nails cut so if you are unsure, enlist the services of your vet or local dog groomer.

Teeth should be cleaned regularly.

Wipe inside the ear, making sure not to probe too deeply.

Debris should be cleared from the eyes.

Trim nails on a routine basis.

Feet

Long hair tends to grow around your Cavalier's feet, and it is fine to leave this in its natural state. In fact, it is frowned upon in the show ring if the Cavalier has his feet trimmed.

However, you need to check the underside of the feet, as hair tends to grow between the pads. This can become dirty and matted, and can cause considerable discomfort to your dog.

The hair should be trimmed on a regular basis, making sure you reward your Cavalier for keeping still while you carry out the procedure.

Exercise

As already discussed, the Cavalier does not require a lot of exercise, but he will thoroughly enjoy it. He will be happy trotting around the garden, but he will also relish a 10-mile hike.

A good walk down the road on the lead is also acceptable – anything that keeps the muscles and joints well used. However, there is no better sight than seeing a Cavalier running at full pelt across a green field, with his ears flowing in the wind!

The older Cavalier

As the years go by your friend will start to get old, and you will probably have to make gradual changes to his daily routine.

Whereas once your Cavalier enjoyed a race round the local park, he may just be happy with a little potter down the road, or round the garden.

You might notice he is no longer able to eat all his food in one go – or indeed crunch it, as he used to. To help him, it is easy enough to soak his food, and also to divide it into two or even three smaller portions, which he may find more manageable.

He may not be able to keep himself quite as clean as he once did, so use baby wipes to clean around his eyes, mouth and maybe his nether regions. His eyesight may deteriorate along with his hearing.

These are all things you will have to make allowances and compensate for. I have actually taught some of my oldies basic sign language for things like 'go in' or 'out' or 'come here' or when their meal is ready. They do adapt quite easily.

Letting go

It is a very painful to know that we will have to say goodbye to our dear friend before we are ready to. But there is, at least, one final service we can do for him, and that is not to let him suffer. It would be so much easier if he just drifted off in his sleep, saving us the pain of making the decision, but this very rarely happens.

Believe me, for all the dogs I have loved and lost over the years, it never gets any easier. I often think of the quote from one of my favorite films, Shadowlands, which helps me: "The pain now is part of the happiness then. That's the deal."

The one thing I make sure I do for all my dogs, is to stay with them until the end, whether the vet comes to the house or I take him to the surgery.

Make sure he can see you. Talk to him and keep stroking him, so as he slips away, the last thing he sees, hears and feels is the person he has loved all his life.

It is natural to grieve but, in time, you will be able to look back and remember all the happy times you spent with your beloved Cavalier.

Social skills

Cavaliers love everyone and everything, and are naturally sociable little dogs. The trouble can be that they think everyone loves them, too, so it is important to teach some social graces.

The outside world

Once your Cavalier has settled into his new home and completed his vaccinations, he will be ready to go into the outside world. Like all young dogs, a Cavalier needs to be exposed to a wide range of different situations so he learns to react calmly and confidently.

- Allow your Cavalier to meet people of all ages in different environments. He needs to greet visitors – both friends and strangers – that come to your house. When he is out on walks, he should get used to seeing people in hats, carrying umbrellas, and riding bicycles.

- Take your Cavalier to quiet areas to begin with and progress to busier areas – with more people and more traffic – as he grows in confidence.

- If your Cavalier appears hesitant, or even frightened, do not try to comfort him or he will think there is really something to worry about. Instead, adopt a calm, no-nonsense approach, and distract the pup with a treat. Then move on, giving him lots of verbal encouragement.

- Do not pull him towards the thing he is frightened of; give him a chance to work out that it is not scary, and allow him to walk past at some distance so that he gains in confidence.

Meeting other dogs

There will be plenty of places to socialize your puppy. Your vet may organize puppy parties, or be able to put you in touch with a training club. You will not be able to take him to any of these before he is vaccinated, but this should not be detrimental to a happy, healthy, well-reared puppy.

Make sure everything you do with your puppy at these events is a positive experience. Anything negative you do will exacerbate the situation. For example, if another dog comes charging over in a friendly but over exuberant manner, do not be tempted to sweep your pup up into your arms – that will only teach him to be frightened of this kind of approach. Let him deal with it by himself. Doing this will actually encourage him to grow in confidence.

Let your Cavalier approach other dogs, on the lead. In this way you can control how much they interact and suppress anything he does that might be a little over the top. Some dogs will not welcome the advances of a friendly, enthusiastic Cavalier puppy and may react aggressively, so don't take liberties.

Keep taking your Cavalier along to classes to reinforce what he has learnt, so his personality and disposition can continue to grow and flourish, as it should.

Training
guidelines

When you are training it will help
to have some guidelines which will
increase your chances of success.

- Find a reward your Cavalier really wants. This
  could be a toy or a tasty treat. You can vary the
  reward so you have high value treats (cheese or
  sausage) for teaching new exercises and recalls
  away from home, and low value treats (dry kibble)
  for routine training.

- Work on your tone of voice. This will be far more
  meaningful to your Cavalier than the words you
  are saying. Use a bright, happy, upbeat tone when
  you are training, and a deep, firm voice when
  you catch him red-handed – raiding the bin, for
  example. Go over the top when you are praising
  your Cavalier so that he understands how pleased
  you are with him.

- Train in short sessions. This applies particularly to
  puppies that have a very short attention span, but
  adults will also switch off if sessions are too long.

- Never train if you are preoccupied or if you are
  in a bad mood. Your Cavalier will pick up on your
  negative vibes, and the session is doomed to
  disaster.

- Teach one lesson at a time and only proceed to the next lesson when the first has been mastered.

Progress in small steps so your Cavalier understands what you want him to do.

- Praise success lavishly and ignore failure. If your Cavalier gets something wrong, do not reprimand him. Simply ignore what he has done and try again. This will give you the opportunity to praise him if he gets it right. If he is still struggling, break the exercise into stages, so he understands more clearly, and you can reward his success a step at a time.

- Make sure training sessions always end on a positive note – even if this means abandoning an exercise for the time being and finishing with something you know your Cavalier can do.

Above all, make sure your training sessions are fun, with lots of play and plenty of opportunities to reward your Cavalier.

First lessons

Cavaliers are keen to learn and eager to please. Do not delay in starting training as it is far easier to instil good habits than to break bad habits.

Wearing a collar

It is never too early to get your puppy used to wearing his collar. Give him a day or two to settle in his new home, and then try putting it on, making sure it is fitted correctly. You should be able to fit the width of two fingers under the collar without it being too slack.

Your pup will probably start to scratch at his neck quite persistently. Don't worry about this, it is perfectly normal. It is purely because of the strange feeling of having something round his neck for the first time. This should only last a few days – a week at most.

Lead training

When your Cavalier is used to wearing his collar, you can start lead training. Start by clipping the lead on

to the collar and letting him walk round dragging it with him, making sure it does not become snarled up. That will allow him to get used to the weight of the lead and the feel of it on his neck.

Now take him out in the garden and start to put a little pressure on. Just gently hold the lead so he will feel a bit of restraint from it. He may object, but persevere using some treats to distract him. The trick is 'little and often', making sure you give him lots of praise when he co-operates.

When your Cavalier is happy to have his lead on, and accepts that you hold on to it, you can take the next and final step – getting him to walk on the lead. Hold the lead loosely and, armed with a tasty treat, encourage him to follow you. As long as he is walking with you, encourage and praise him lavishly.

If he should suddenly start to fight against the lead, do not let the lead go. If you do, your pup will think that he just has to throw a tantrum to get his own way.

Ignore him until he is calm, and then try again. It should not take more than a few days to get him walking on the lead. After that, it is simply a matter of practicing, and rewarding success, so that your Cavalier learns that walking by your side, on a loose lead, is the best place to be.

Facing page:
The aim is for your Cavalier to walk on a loose lead, neither pulling ahead nor lagging behind.

Come when called

Teaching a reliable recall is invaluable for both you and your Cavalier. You are secure in the knowledge that he will come back when he is called, and your Cav benefits from being allowed free-running exercise.

Your puppy may have learned to "Come" in the confined space of your kitchen – and this is a good place to build up a positive association with the verbal cue – particularly if you ask your puppy to "Come" to get his dinner!

The next stage is to transfer the lesson to the garden. Arm yourself with some treats, and wait until your puppy is distracted. Then call him, using a higher-pitched, excited tone of voice. If your puppy responds, immediately reward him with a treat. If he is slow to come, run away a few steps and then call again, making yourself sound really exciting. Jump up and down, open your arms wide to welcome him; it doesn't matter how silly you look, he needs to see you as the most fun person in the world.

Now you are ready to introduce some distractions. Try calling him when someone else is in the garden, or wait a few minutes until he is investigating a really interesting scent. When he responds, make a really big fuss of him and give him some extra treats so he knows it is worth his while to come to you.

When you have a reliable recall in the garden, you can venture into the outside world. Do not be too ambitious to begin with; try a recall in a quiet place with the minimum of distractions and only progress to more challenging environments if your Cavalier is responding well.

Do not make the mistake of only asking your dog to come at the end of a walk. What is the incentive in coming back to you if all you do is clip on his lead and head for home? Instead, call your dog at random times throughout the walk, giving him a treat and a stroke, and then letting him go free again. In this way, coming to you is always rewarding, and does not signal the end of his free run.

Stationary exercises

These are easy exercises to teach, and you and your Cavalier will enjoy some fairly instant success!

Sit

This is best taught with a lure, which can be a treat or a toy, although most people find that using a treat is easier.

- Show your Cavalier you have a treat and hold it just above his nose.

- As he looks up at the treat, he will go into the sit position. Reward him immediately.

- Keep practicing and when your Cavalier understands what you want, introduce the verbal cue, "Sit".

You can practice this exercise at mealtimes, holding the food bowl above his head, and waiting for him to sit before putting it down.

Down

You can start with your dog in a Sit or a Stand for this exercise.

- Stand or kneel in front of him and show him you have a treat in your hand. Hold the treat just in front of his nose and slowly lower it towards the ground, between his front legs.

- As he follows the treat he will go down on his front legs and, in a few moments, his hindquarters will follow.

- Close your hand over the treat so your Cavalier doesn't cheat and get the treat before he is in the correct position. As soon as he is in the Down, give him the treat and lots of praise.

- Keep practicing, and when your Cavalier understands what you want, introduce the verbal cue "Down".

Control exercises

These may not be the most exciting of exercises but they introduce control which will help to keep your Cavalier safe in all situations.

Wait

This exercise teaches your Cavalier to "Wait" in position until you give the next command; it differs from the Stay exercise in which your Cav must stay where you have left him for a more prolonged period.

The most useful application of "Wait" is when you are getting your dog out of the car and you need him to stay in position until you clip on his lead.

Start with your puppy on the lead to give you a greater chance of success. Ask him to "Sit" as you stand in front of him.

Step back one pace, holding your hand, palm flat, facing him. Wait a second and then come back to stand in front of him. You can then reward him and release him with a word, such as "OK". Practice this a few times, gradually increasing the distance and the time you can leave your Cavalier, and then introduce the verbal cue "Wait".

You can reinforce the lesson by using it in different situations, such as asking your Cavalier to "Wait" before you put his food bowl down, or before you throw his toy.

Stay

You need to differentiate this exercise by using a different hand signal and a different verbal cue.

Start with your Cavalier in the Down as he is most likely to be secure in this position. Stand by his side and then step forwards, with your hand held back, palm facing the dog.

Step back, release him, and then reward him. Practice until your Cav understands the exercise and then introduce the verbal cue "Stay".

Gradually increase the distance you can leave your puppy, and increase the challenge by walking around him – and even stepping over him – so that he learns he must "Stay" until you release him.

Do not try to run before you can walk by extending the distance you leave him too quickly. Your Cavalier needs to grasp the concept of staying in position until you test him.

It is easiest to teach the "Stay" when your Cavalier is in the Down position.

Leave

Leave is a useful command to have in your repertoire, as it can be used in a variety of situations. For example, you can use it when he goes to pick something off the street that is highly undesirable, when he is tempted to chase the neighbor's cat, or even when he is too enthusiastic in greeting a member of the family.

It should be a short and fairly sharp rebuff – "Leave" followed by bags of praise and a treat when he does follow the command. Using a firm voice gives you authority, and the instant he responds, you can reward him. In this way, he learns that it more rewarding to obey the verbal cue "Leave" than to follow his own desires.

Opportunities for Cavaliers

If you are enjoying training your Cavalier, you may want to get involved in more advanced training, or take part in one of the many canine sports on offer.

The show ring

If you intend to show your puppy, you will need to attend ringcraft classes so you train your dog to perform in the ring and you can also learn about show ring etiquette

When your Cavalier has learnt how to behave in the ring, you are ready to compete. The first classes are for puppies from six months of age and progress through different categories. There are different types of shows you can attend from informal fun day events to the all-important Championship shows where Cavaliers compete for the prestigious title of Champion.

Showing is great fun, but at the top level it is highly

competitive, so you will need to learn the art of winning – and losing – gracefully.

Good citizen scheme

The Good Citizen Scheme is run by the national Kennel Clubs in both the USA and the UK. It is designed to promote responsible ownership and to teach basic obedience and good manners so your dog is a model citizen in the community.

In the US there is one test; in the UK there are four award levels: Puppy Foundation, Bronze, Silver and Gold.

The exercises include:

- Walking on a loose lead

- Recall amid distractions

- Controlled greeting

- Grooming and handling

- Stays

- Food manners

- Sendaway.

Obedience

If your Cavalier has mastered basic obedience, you may want to get involved in competitive obedience. The exercises include: heelwork at varying paces with dog and handler following a pattern decided by the judge, stays, recalls, retrieves, sendaways, scent discrimination and distance control. The exercises get progressively harder as you progress up the classes.

A Cavalier will readily learn the exercises that are used in obedience competitions, but, at the top level, a very high degree of precision and accuracy is called for, which some Cavaliers may find too exacting.

Agility

This is great fun to watch and join in. Against the clock, at the fastest speed they can muster, dogs jump over obstacles, through tires and tunnels, and negotiate the contact equipment, which includes an A frame, a dog walk and a seesaw.

The Cavalier competes in classes for small dogs, where the height of the jumps is reduced. They are fast, agile and responsive, and many Cavaliers have proved very successful in this discipline.

Dancing with dogs

This sport is becoming increasingly popular and the Cavalier thrives on the challenge. Dog and handler must perform a choreographed routine to music, which includes a variety of tricks and moves. Routines are judged on style, presentation, content and accuracy.

Health care

We are fortunate that the Cavalier is a healthy dog, and with good routine care, a well-balanced diet, and sufficient exercise, most will experience few health problems.

However, it is your responsibility to put a program of preventative health care in place – and this should start from the moment your puppy, or older dog, arrives in his new home.

Vaccinations

Dogs are subject to a number of contagious diseases. In the old days, these were killers, and resulted in heartbreak for many owners. Vaccinations have now been developed, and the occurrence of the major infectious diseases is now very rare. However, this will only remain the case if all pet owners follow a strict policy of vaccinating their dogs.

There are vaccinations available for the following diseases:

Adenovirus: This affects the liver; affected dogs have a classic 'blue eye'.

Distemper: A viral disease which causes chest and

gastro-intestinal damage. The brain may also be affected, leading to fits and paralysis.

Parvovirus: Causes severe gastro enteritis, and most commonly affects puppies.

Leptospirosis: This bacterial disease is carried by rats and affects many mammals, including humans. It causes liver and kidney damage.

Rabies: A virus that affects the nervous system and is invariably fatal. The first signs are abnormal behavior when the infected dog may bite another animal or a person. Paralysis and death follow. Vaccination is compulsory in most countries. In the UK, dogs travelling overseas must be vaccinated.

Kennel Cough: There are several strains of Kennel Cough, but they all result in a harsh, dry, cough. This disease is rarely fatal; in fact, most dogs make a good recovery within a matter of weeks and show few signs of ill health while they are affected. However, kennel cough is highly infectious among dogs that live together so, for this reason, most boarding kennels will insist that your dog is protected by the vaccine, given as nose drops.

Lyme Disease: This is a bacterial disease transmitted by ticks (see page 164). The first signs are limping, but the heart, kidneys and nervous system can also be affected. The ticks that transmit the disease occur in specific regions, such as the north-east states of the USA, some of the southern states, California and the upper Mississippi region. Lyme disease is still rare in the UK so vaccinations are not routinely offered.

Vaccination program

In the UK, vaccinations are routinely given for distemper, adenovirus, leptospirosis and parvovirus. In the USA, the American Animal Hospital Association advises vaccination for core diseases, which they list as: distemper, adenovirus, parvovirus and rabies. The requirement for vaccinating for non-core diseases – leptospirosis, lyme disease and kennel cough – should be assessed depending on a dog's individual risk and his likely exposure to the disease.

In most cases, a puppy will start his vaccinations at around eight weeks of age, with the second part given a fortnight later. However, this does vary depending on the individual policy of veterinary practices, and the incidence of disease in your area.

You should also talk to your vet about whether to give annual booster vaccinations. This depends on an individual dog's levels of immunity, and how long a particular vaccine remains effective.

Parasites

No matter how well you look after your Cavalier, you will have to accept that parasites – internal and external – are ever present, and you need to take preventative action.

Internal parasites: As the name suggests, these parasites live inside your dog. Most will find a home in the digestive tract, but there is also a parasite that lives in the heart. If infestation is unchecked, a dog's health will be severely jeopardized, but routine preventative treatment is simple and effective.

External parasites: These parasites live on your dog's body – in his skin and fur, and sometimes in his ears.

Roundworm

This is found in the small intestine. Signs of infestation will be a poor coat, a pot belly, diarrhoea and lethargy. Pregnant mothers should be treated, but it is almost inevitable that parasites will be passed on to the puppies. For this reason, a breeder will start a worming program, which you will need to continue. Ask your vet for advice on treatment, which will need to continue throughout your dog's life.

Tapeworm

Infection occurs when fleas and lice are ingested; the adult worm takes up residence in the small intestine, releasing mobile segments (which contain eggs) which can be seen in a dog's feces as small rice-like grains. The only other obvious sign of infestation is irritation of the anus. Again, routine preventative treatment is required throughout your Cavalier's life.

Heartworm

This parasite is transmitted by mosquitoes, and so will only occur where these insects thrive. A warm environment is needed for the parasite to develop, so it is more likely to be present in areas with a warm, humid climate. However, it is found in all parts of the USA, although its prevalence does vary. At present, heartworm is rarely seen in the UK.

Heartworms live in the right side of the heart and larvae can grow up to 14 in (35 cm) in length. A dog with heartworm is at severe risk from heart failure, so preventative treatment, as advised by your vet, is essential. Dogs living in the USA should also have regular tests to check for the presence of infection.

Lungworm

Lungworm, or *Angiostrongylus vasorum*, is a parasite that lives in the heart and major blood vessels supplying the lungs. It can cause many problems, such as breathing difficulties, excessive bleeding, sickness and diarrhoea, seizures, and can even be fatal. The parasite is carried by slugs and snails, and the dog becomes infected when ingesting these, often accidentally when rummaging through undergrowth. Lungworm is not common, but it is on the increase and a responsible owner should be aware of it. Fortunately, it is easily preventable and even affected dogs usually make a full recovery if treated early enough. Your vet will be able to advise you on the risks in your area and what form of treatment may be required.

Fleas

A dog may carry dog fleas, cat fleas, and even human fleas. The flea stays on the dog only long enough to have a blood meal and to breed, but its presence will result in itching and scratching. If your dog has an allergy to fleas – which is usually a reaction to the flea's saliva – he will scratch himself until he is raw.

Spot-on treatment, which should be administered on a routine basis, is easy to use and highly effective on all types of fleas. You can also treat your dog with a spray or with insecticidal shampoo. Bear in mind that the whole environment your dog lives in will need to be sprayed, and all other pets living in your home will also need to be treated.

How to detect fleas

You may suspect your dog has fleas, but how can you be sure? There are two methods to try.

Run a fine comb through your dog's coat, and see if you can detect the presence of fleas on the skin, or clinging to the comb. Alternatively, sit your dog on some white paper and rub his back. This will dislodge feces from the fleas, which will be visible as small brown specks. To double check, shake the specks on to some damp cotton wool (cotton). Flea feces consists of the dried blood taken from the host, so if the specks turn a lighter shade of red, you know your dog has fleas.

Ticks

These are blood-sucking parasites which are most frequently found in rural areas where sheep or deer are present. The main danger is their ability to pass lyme disease to both dogs and humans. Lyme disease is prevalent in some areas of the USA (see page 158), although it is still rare in the UK. The treatment you give your dog for fleas generally works for ticks, but you should discuss the best product to use with your vet.

How to remove a tick

If you spot a tick on your dog, do not try to pluck it off as you risk leaving the hard mouth parts embedded in his skin. The best way to remove a tick is to use a fine pair of tweezers or you can buy a tick remover. Grasp the tick head firmly and then pull the tick straight out from the skin. If you are using a tick remover, check the instructions, as some recommend a circular twist when pulling. When you have removed the tick, clean the area with mild soap and water.

Ear mites

These parasites live in the outer ear canal. The signs of infestation are a brown, waxy discharge, and your dog will continually shake his head and scratch his ear. If you suspect your Cavalier has ear mites, a visit to the vet will be needed so that medicated ear drops can be prescribed.

Fur mites

These small, white parasites are visible to the naked eye and are often referred to as 'walking dandruff'. They cause a scurfy coat and mild itchiness. However, they are zoonotic – transferable to humans – so prompt treatment with an insecticide prescribed by your vet is essential.

Harvest mites

These are picked up from the undergrowth, and can be seen as a bright orange patch on the webbing between the toes, although this can also be found elsewhere on the body, such as on the ear flaps. Treatment is effective with the appropriate insecticide.

Skin mites

There are two types of parasite that burrow into a dog's skin. *Demodex canis* is transferred from a mother to her pups while they are feeding. Treatment is with a topical preparation, and sometimes antibiotics are needed.

The other skin mite is *sarcoptes scabiei*, which causes intense itching and hair loss. It is highly contagious, so all dogs in a household will need to be treated, which involves repeated bathing with a medicated shampoo.

Common ailments

As with all living animals, dogs can be affected by a variety of ailments, most of which can be treated effectively after consulting with your vet, who will prescribe appropriate medication and will advise you on how to care for your dog's needs.

Here are some of the more common problems that could affect your Cavalier, with advice on how to deal with them.

Anal glands

These are two small sacs on either side of the anus. They produce a dark-brown secretion which dogs use when they mark their territory. The anal glands should empty every time a dog defecates but if they become blocked or impacted, a dog will experience increasing discomfort. He may nibble at his rear end, or 'scoot' his bottom along the ground to relieve the irritation.

Treatment involves a trip to the vet, who will empty the glands manually. It is important to do this without delay or infection may occur.

Back/neck problems

Often just a temporary problem, due to a pulled muscle, but Cavaliers can suffer from disc extrusions – slipped discs. Disc disease is usually seen as a sudden onset of back or neck pain with signs of nervous behavior, lack of co-ordination, problems with movement and, in the most severe cases, you may see paralysis.

Veterinary investigation is required and usually involves X-rays of the spine and possibly more sophisticated diagnostic techniques may be necessary (MRI or CT scans). Treatment depends on severity and may include administration of anti-inflammatory drugs and rest. More severe cases may require surgery.

Dental problems

Good dental hygiene will do much to minimize problems with gum infection and tooth decay. If tartar accumulates to the extent that you cannot remove it by brushing, the vet will need to intervene. In a situation such as this, an anesthetic will need to be administered so the tartar can be removed manually.

Diarrhoea

There are many reasons why a dog has diarrhoea, but most commonly it is the result of scavenging, a sudden change of diet, or an adverse reaction to a particular type of food.

If your dog is suffering from diarrhoea, the first step is to withdraw food for a day. It is important that he does not dehydrate, so make sure that fresh drinking water is available. However, drinking too much can increase the diarrhoea, which may be accompanied with vomiting, so limit how much he drinks at any one time.

After allowing the stomach to rest, feed a bland diet, such as white fish or chicken with boiled rice, for a few days. In most cases, your dog's motions will return to normal and you can resume normal feeding, although this should be done gradually.

However, if this fails to work and the diarrhoea persists for more than a few days, you should consult you vet. Your dog may have an infection, which needs to be treated with antibiotics, or the diarrhoea may indicate some other problem which needs expert diagnosis.

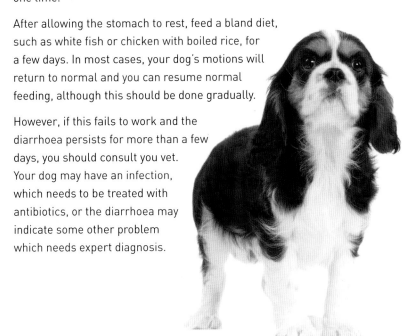

Ear infections

The Cavalier's ears lie close to his head so air cannot circulate as freely as it would in a dog with semi-pricked or pricked ears. Therefore, it is important to keep a close check on your Cavalier's ears.

A healthy ear is clean with no sign of redness or inflammation, and no evidence of a waxy brown discharge or a foul odor. If you see your dog scratching his ear, shaking his head, or holding one ear at an odd angle, you will need to consult your vet.

The most likely causes are ear mites (see page 164), an infection, or there may a foreign body, such as a grass seed, trapped in the ear.

Depending on the cause, treatment is with medicated ear drops, possibly containing antibiotics. If a foreign body is suspected, the vet will need to carry our further investigations.

Eye problems

The Cavalier has large, round eyes, and though they should not protrude, they are more prone to injury than is the case with some other breeds.

If your Cavalier's eyes look red and sore, he may be suffering from conjunctivitis. This may, or may not be accompanied by a watery or a crusty discharge.

Conjunctivitis can be caused by a bacterial or viral infection, it could be the result
of an injury, or it could be an adverse reaction to pollen.

You will need to consult your vet for a correct diagnosis, but in the case of an infection, treatment with medicated eye drops is effective.

Conjunctivitis may also be the first sign of more serious inherited eye problems (see page 188).

Foreign bodies

In the home, puppies – and some older dogs – cannot resist chewing anything that looks interesting.

The toys you choose for your dog should be suitably robust to withstand damage, but children's toys can be irresistible. Some dogs will chew – and swallow – anything from socks, tights, and any other items from the laundry basket to golf balls and stones from the garden.

Obviously, these items are indigestible and could cause an obstruction in your dog's intestine, which is potentially lethal.

The signs to look for are vomiting, and a tucked up posture. The dog will often be restless and will look as though he is in pain.

In this situation, you must get your dog to the vet without delay as surgery will be needed to remove the obstruction.

Heatstroke

The Cavalier enjoys his exercise, but care should be taken on hot days as heatstroke is a potential danger. When the temperature rises, make sure your dog always has access to shady areas, and wait for a cooler part of the day before going for a walk.

Be extra careful if you leave your Cavalier in the car, as the temperature can rise dramatically – even on a cloudy day. Heatstroke can happen very rapidly, and unless you are able lower your dog's temperature, it can be fatal.

If your Cavalier appears to be suffering from heatstroke, lie him flat and then cool him as quickly as possible by hosing him, covering him with wet towels, or using frozen food bags from the freezer. As soon as he has made some recovery, take him to the vet where cold intravenous fluids can be administered.

Lameness/limping

There are a wide variety of reasons why a dog can go lame, from a simple muscle strain, to a fracture, ligament damage, or more complex problems with the joints which may be an inherited disorder (see pages 180). It takes an expert to make a correct diagnosis, so if you are concerned about your dog, do not delay in seeking help.

The Cavalier, in common with many other toy breeds, is susceptible to having knee-caps (patellae) that appear to be loose and that will move (or dislocate) to one side out of their natural groove. The condition is fairly common and whilst it is undesirable to breed from an affected dog, it is not always associated with lameness.

As your Cavalier becomes more elderly, he may suffer from arthritis, which you will see as general stiffness, particularly when he gets up after resting. It will help if you ensure his bed is in a warm draught-free location, and if your Cavalier gets wet after exercise, you must dry him thoroughly.

If your elderly Cavalier seems to be in pain, consult your vet who will be able to help with pain relief medication.

Skin problems

If your dog is scratching or nibbling at his skin, the first thing to check is that he is free from fleas (see page 162). There are other external parasites which cause itching and hair loss, but you will need a vet to help you find the culprit.

An allergic reaction is another major cause of skin problems. It can be quite an undertaking to find the cause of the allergy, and you will need to follow your vet's advice, which often requires eliminating specific ingredients from the diet, as well as looking at environmental factors.

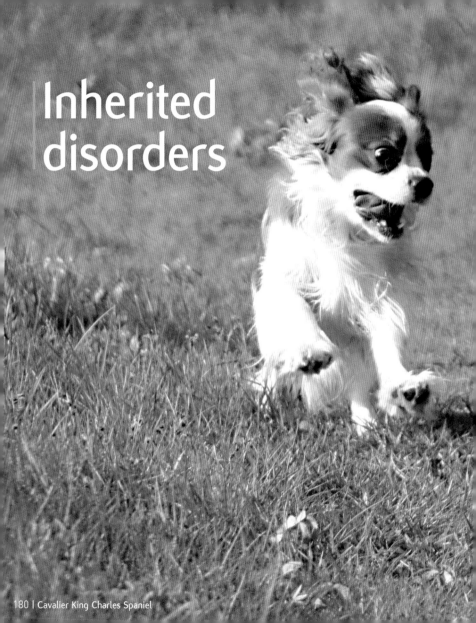

Inherited
disorders

The Cavalier King Charles Spaniel has a number of conditions that are recognized as being inherited within the breed. There are now screening tests to enable breeders to check for affected individuals which are then eliminated from breeding programs, thereby reducing the prevalence of these diseases within the breed.

DNA testing is also becoming more widely available, and as research into different genetic diseases progresses, more DNA tests are being developed.

Heart disease

Mitral valve disease (MVD) is relatively common in Cavaliers but, in many cases, the affected dog may not show any functional impairment for many years. Once clinical signs do appear, medication will be required and this is likely to be necessary for the remainder of the dog's life.

Early signs may include increased panting, coughing or tiring easily whilst out on walks, or following over-exertion in hot weather. However, many dogs live for years with heart problems and, while dogs known to be affected should not be used for breeding, such animals can continue to lead happy lives for a long time.

The condition is caused by a physical defect in the mitral valve located in the heart, which results in blood being pumped inefficiently. In severe cases it may cause a build-up of fluid in the chest, resulting in coughing, and collapse as the muscles are deprived of well-oxygenated blood. Heart medications have greatly improved over the last decade and are now much safer and can be given for long periods without undue complications.

Syringomyelia (SM), Occipital hypoplasia or Chiari-like malformation (CM)

The Cavalier is one of the breeds most well known to have the potential to suffer from SM/CM and the syndrome is thought to be inherited. Chiari-like malformation (CM), a term derived from human medicine, is also known as occipital hypoplasia.

This is a malformation of the rear part of the dog's skull, affecting the occipital bone.

In simple terms, there are structural defects such that the rear part of the brain seems to be too large for the rear part of the skull that should contain it. This means part of the brain (cerebellum) may be forced slightly out of the back of the skull through the large hole in the skull (the foramen magnum) through which the brain connects with the spinal cord.

Syringomyelia is a condition where there is an abnormality – a fluid-filled cavity (or syrinx) within the spinal cord tissue. It is usually seen in dogs with CM and is possibly caused by an abnormal flow of cerebrospinal fluid between the brain and the spinal cord through the now-blocked foramen magnum. The expansion of the cavity, or syrinx, results in irreversible damage to the nervous system. The larger the dilation, the more likely and obvious are the abnormal clinical signs. While not all cases of SM have cerebellar herniation, there is a high association between the two, and most cases of SM appear to be secondary to CM, although there may be other causes.

SM results in varying degrees of problems for affected animals, from those dogs that show no abnormal signs to some animals that have a lot of

damage to the spinal cord and show abnormalities by a year old. Symptoms are usually first seen in affected individuals between the age of five months and three years, although they can show up at any age. Signs that are commonly seen in dogs with SM may include:

- Scratching of the neck, shoulder or ear. The dog often only scratches at one side of the body, particularly while walking. Sometimes the scratching motion doesn't actually make contact with the body.

- Signs of discomfort or pain in the head or neck, such as crying. Neck pain is often intermittent, rather than a continuous pain, particularly at first.

- Scoliosis – a bend in the neck to one side.

- Weakness of the legs, or a wobbly gait (ataxia).

- Occasionally paralysis of facial muscles or deafness may be associated with SM.

While the condition might be suspected if a Cavalier shows some of the characteristic clinical signs, it can only be properly diagnosed by use of magnetic resonance imaging (MRI). There has been work trying to develop a genetic test for the condition, although this has not yet proved successful.

Some cases of SM are so mild that they go undiagnosed, or no treatment is required. In other cases, drugs can help control the signs. In more severe cases, drugs may not control the pain or nervous signs and surgery to reduce the constriction is sometimes attempted, although this is not always successful.

Eye conditions

There are a number of eye conditions affecting dogs of almost all breeds that can be inherited. Testing is carried out by the Canine Eye Registration Foundation in the US; in the UK there is a combined scheme run by the British Veterinary Association, the Kennel Club and the International Sheep Dog Society.

Eye conditions known to be inherited in Cavaliers include:

Microphthalmia: very small eyes with associated defects present at birth.

Distichiasis: presence of abnormal eyelashes on the eyelids that rub on the surface of the eye causing discomfort.

Entropion: abnormal eyelids that roll inwards and rub on the eye causing discomfort.

Corneal dystrophy: a whitish appearance of the eye due to abnormalities of the cornea, usually affecting both eyes.

Exposure keratopathy: this is a condition of the cornea resulting from inadequate blinking.

Cataract: may affect one or both eyes and presents as an opacity of the lens causing partial or complete blindness.

Multifocal retinal dysplasia: abnormal development of the retina present at birth associated with visual impairment.

Hip dysplasia

Although a common inherited problem for many breeds hip dysplasia is not a major problem for Cavaliers, but a testing scheme is available for use if desired.

Epilepsy

Although uncommon, idiopathic epilepsy (fits) is an inheritable disease in Cavaliers and, where suspected, it is desirable to avoid breeding from affected lines.

Summing up

It may give the pet owner cause for concern to find about health problems that may affect their dog. But it is important to bear in mind that acquiring some basic knowledge is an asset, as it will allow you to spot signs of trouble at an early stage. Early diagnosis is very often the means to the most effective treatment.

Fortunately, the Cavalier is a generally healthy and disease-free dog with his only visits to the vet being annual check-ups. In most cases, owners can look forward to enjoying many happy years with this loyal companion.

Useful addresses

Breed & Kennel Clubs
Please contact your Kennel Club to obtain contact information about breed clubs in your area.

UK
The Kennel Club (UK)
1 Clarges Street London, W1J 8AB
Telephone: 0870 606 6750
Fax: 0207 518 1058
Web: www.thekennelclub.org.uk

USA
American Kennel Club (AKC)
5580 Centerview Drive, Raleigh, NC 27606.
Telephone: 919 233 9767
Fax: 919 233 3627
Email: info@akc.org
Web: www.akc.org

United Kennel Club (UKC)
100 E Kilgore Rd, Kalamazoo,
MI 49002-5584, USA.
Tel: 269 343 9020
Fax: 269 343 7037
Web:www.ukcdogs.com/

Australia
Australian National Kennel Council (ANKC)
The Australian National Kennel Council is the administrative body for pure breed canine affairs in Australia. It does not, however, deal directly with dog exhibitors, breeders or judges. For information pertaining to breeders, clubs or shows, please contact the relevant State or Territory Body.

International
Fédération Cynologique Internationalé (FCI)
Place Albert 1er, 13, B-6530 Thuin, Belgium.
Tel: +32 71 59.12.38
Fax: +32 71 59.22.29
Web: www.fci.be/

Training and behavior
UK
Association of Pet Dog Trainers
Telephone: 01285 810811
Web: http://www.apdt.co.uk

Association of Pet Behaviour Counsellors
Telephone: 01386 751151
Web: http://www.apbc.org.uk/

USA
Association of Pet Dog Trainers
Tel: 1 800 738 3647
Web: www.apdt.com/

American College of Veterinary Behaviorists
Web: http://dacvb.org/

American Veterinary Society of Animal Behavior
Web: www.avsabonline.org/

Australia
APDT Australia Inc
Web: www.apdt.com.au

Canine Behavior
For details of regional behaviorists, contact the relevant State or Territory Controlling Body.

Activities

UK
Agility Club
http://www.agilityclub.co.uk/

British Flyball Association
Telephone: 01628 829623
Web: http://www.flyball.org.uk/

USA
North American Dog Agility Council
Web: www.nadac.com/

North American Flyball Association, Inc.
Tel/Fax: 800 318 6312
Web: www.flyball.org/

Australia
Agility Dog Association of Australia
Tel: 0423 138 914
Web: www.adaa.com.au/

NADAC Australia
Web: www.nadacaustralia.com/

Australian Flyball Association
Tel: 0407 337 939
Web: www.flyball.org.au/

International
World Canine Freestyle Organisation
Tel: (718) 332-8336
Web: www.worldcaninefreestyle.org

Health

UK
British Small Animal Veterinary
Association
Tel: 01452 726700
Web: http://www.bsava.com/

Royal College of Veterinary Surgeons
Tel: 0207 222 2001
Web: www.rcvs.org.uk

Alternative Veterinary Medicine Centre
Tel: 01367 710324
Web: www.alternativevet.org/

USA
American Veterinary Medical Association
Tel: 800 248 2862
Web: www.avma.org

American College of Veterinary Surgeons
Tel: 301 916 0200
Toll Free: 877 217 2287
Web: www.acvs.org/

Canine Eye Registration Foundation
The Veterinary Medical DataBases
1717 Philo Rd, PO Box 3007,
Urbana, IL 61803-3007
Tel: 217-693-4800
Fax: 217-693-4801
Web: http://www.vmdb.org/cerf.html

Orthopaedic Foundation of Animals
2300 E Nifong Boulevard
Columbia, Missouri, 65201-3806
Tel: 573 442-0418
Fax: 573 875-5073
Web: http://www.offa.org/

American Holistic Veterinary Medical
Association
Tel: 410 569 0795
Web: www.ahvma.org/

Australia
Australian Small Animal Veterinary
Association
Tel: 02 9431 5090
Web: www.asava.com.au

Australian Veterinary Association
Tel: 02 9431 5000
Web: www.ava.com.au

Australian College Veterinary Scientists
Tel: 07 3423 2016
Web: http://acvsc.org.au

Australian Holistic Vets
Web: www.ahv.com.au/